PLATFORM PAPERS

QUARTERLY ESSAYS ON THE PERFORMING ARTS FROM CURRENCY HOUSE

No. 57
November 2018

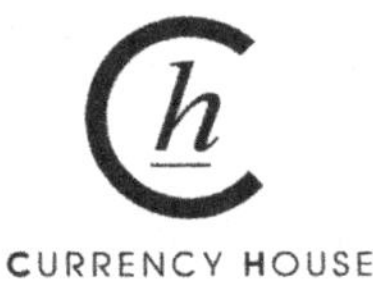

CURRENCY HOUSE

Platform Papers Partners

We acknowledge with gratitude our Partners in continuing support of Platform Papers and its mission to widen understanding of performing arts practice and encourage change when it is needed:

Neil Armfield, AO
Anita Luca Belgiorno-Nettis Foundation
Andrew Bovell
Katharine Brisbane, AM
Elizabeth Butcher, AM
Penny Chapman
Robert Connolly
Dr Peter Cooke, AM
Sally Crawford
Wesley Enoch
Ferrier Hodgson
Larry Galbraith
Wayne Harrison, AM
Campbell Hudson
Lindy Hume
Professors Bruce King and Denise Bradley, AC
Justice François Kunc
Dr Richard Letts, AM
Peter Lowry, OAM and Carolyn Lowry, OAM
David Marr
Helen O'Neil
Martin Portus
Lesley Power
Professor William Purcell
Queensland Performing Arts Centre Trust
Geoffrey Rush, AC
Dr Merilyn Sleigh
Maisy Stapleton
Augusta Supple
Christopher Tooher
Caroline Verge
Rachel Ward, AM and Bryan Brown, AM
Kim Williams, AM
Professor Di Yerbury, AM
Queensland Performing Arts Trust

And we welcome our
MAJOR CORPORATE
SPONSOR FOR 2018

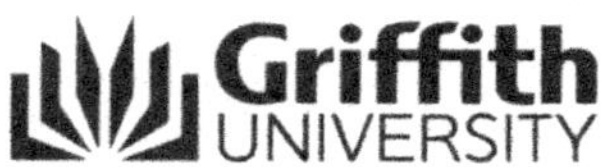

To them and to all subscribers and Friends of Currency House we extend our grateful thanks.

Platform Papers Readers' Forum

Readers' responses to our previous essays are posted on our website. Contributions to the conversation (250 to 2000 words) may be emailed to info@currencyhouse.org.au. The Editor welcomes opinion and criticism in the interest of healthy debate but reserves the right to monitor where necessary.

Platform Papers, quarterly essays on the performing arts, is published every February, May, August and November and is available through bookshops, by subscription and online in paper or electronic version. For details see our website at www.currencyhouse.org.au.

CULTURAL JUSTICE AND THE RIGHT TO THRIVE

SCOTT RANKIN

ABOUT THE AUTHOR

SCOTT RANKIN grew up living on an unlicensed Chinese Junk on Sydney's Lane Cove River with his parents, two sisters, a grandmother and two ducks. This creative way of life continued until he turned sixteen and the family was evicted. Suburbia disagreed with him and Scott completed school hoping to escape via Sydney College of the Arts, which, in turn, filled him with despair. He is now completing his PhD at Queensland University of Technology. Scott learned to love words but they wouldn't stay on the page, so he wrote them to be spoken. These performances made people laugh and cry and he soon found himself collaborating on shows that made money. But by this time his passion for social justice was gaining the upper hand. The two came together in Big *h*ART.

Scott Rankin has been the Creative Director of Australia's leading campaigning arts organisation Big *h*ART for the past 26 years. His projects have been included in the Sydney, Melbourne, Adelaide, Perth, Brisbane, Ten Days on the Island and Edinburgh festivals, and the company has toured to Dublin, London, Netherlands, Sweden, Iceland, South Africa, New Zealand and Germany. Scott's collaborative theatre works include *Namatjira*, *Tjaabi – Flood Country*, *Blue*

Angel, *Hipbone Sticking Out*, *Ngapartji Ngapartji*, *Box The Pony*, *Stickybricks*, *The Northcott Project*, *Certified Male*, *Kissing Frogs*; and he has provided creative and executive support for many of Big *h*ART's award-winning films, *DRIVE* (ABC1), *Nothing Rhymes with Ngapartji* (ABC1), *Hurt* (SBS), *Knot@Home* (eight-part SBS documentary series), *900 Neighbours* (ABC1) and *Namatjira* (ABC1).

Big *h*ART has worked in over 50 communities, and under Scott's creative direction has received 45 awards, including the 2017 Telstra Business Award of the Year and Charity of the Year in Tasmania; a World Health Organisation award, an AFI award, eight National Institute of Criminology Violence Prevention awards, and the Myer Performing Arts Group Award. In 2018 Scott was named the Tasmanian of the Year.

Scott is an essayist and frequent public speaker in diverse locations, from prisons and isolated communities to the media and public forums. He lives on Tommeginner Country in far north-west Tasmania.

Acknowledgements

I am passionate about cultural rights. However, they can mean many things to many people and I am grateful to Katharine Brisbane and Martin Portus of Currency House for their considered editorial support in defining them. My thanks go to Deb Myers for assisting me early in the process to make sense of the many ideas and words. For his intellect and help in initiating my PhD, which explores the ideas that flow into this paper, I thank Brad Haseman. For project evaluations over many years, working both separately and together, Peter Wright and Dave Palmer provided a rich background for this writing.

The heart of the paper comes from working with the many project participants who stay in touch, such as Darren Simpson from the first project, who contributes here; and I thank them for what they have taught me. Also my family and friends who put up with long hours and so much travel. I also thank those who have allowed my thinking to develop: my mentor for many decades, Vanessa Crimmins; John Bakes, who co-founded the organisation; and the Big *h*ART Board and many private funders.

I also thank the elders from many traditions who have invited us to work in their communities and helped to hone the approaches outlined in the paper: Ngarluma, Yindjirbarndi, Pitjantjatjara and Western Aranda elders, senior custodians of high Aboriginal culture who advise and keep our many intercultural projects safe. Similarly, there have been many contributions to the company and my thinking from diverse backgrounds—Greek, Japanese, Indian, Afghan and Anglo—settler traditions whose collaborations have shaped my work, and in turn shaped this paper.

The biggest thanks, for their contribution to the thinking behind this paper, must go to the dedicated current and past Big *h*ART teams in the field. My position across these 26 years of practice has given me the chance to archive—in my heart and mind—this diligent and beautiful process that in turn feeds into this paper, shaping its passion and voice.

A quarter of a century should be adequate time to get things right, and yet, such is the complex and responsive nature of the practice, that can never be. The idea of a right way is an arrogant way. And so I'm grateful to the many other leaders in the field for their 'way,' their skill and their eldership, as we are all grateful for those who will continue to contribute to the flow of change into the future.

Introduction: Big hART Beginnings

Brought up in a world of changes
Part time cleaner in a holiday flat
Stare out to sea at the ships at night
No anaesthesia, I'm gonna work on it day to day
No zephyr no light relief it seems
But maybe it's a dream

This is my home
This is my sea
Don't paint it with the future of factories
I want to stay, I feel okay
There's nothing else as perfect
I'll have my way
Brought up in a world of changes

Two children in the harbour
They play their game stormwater drain
Write their contract in the sand, it'll be grey for life
But you can't stop the sun
From shining on and on and getting you there
Tide forever beckons you to leave

But something holds you back
It's not the promise of the swell or a girl
Just a hope that someday someway it'll be okay
So you stop and say

This is my home
This is my sea
Don't paint it with the future of factories
This is my life
this is my right
I'll make it what I want to
I'll stay and I'll fight

'Burnie' by Midnight Oil, *Place Without a Postcard*, 1981

The city of Burnie is on the north-west coast of Tasmania. Burnie is in the poorest electorate in the poorest state in the country. And it provides a lesson in everyone's right to a culture, and the way cultural participation is at the heart of being able to thrive.

But first some Latin and the use of the terms 'culture' and 'cultural rights' throughout this paper:

> *Culture, in its original meaning 'cultura animi' or 'cultivation of the soul' represents the 'all-embracing conglomeration of universal human values that, throughout time, has found expressions in the most variable creations of human genius that are able to elevate, inspire and raise the level of human*

> *consciousness. To reverse the dead-end race of our degrading society, we need to restore the true value of culture, defending it with the proclamation of the Right to Culture as an inalienable right of every human being, and humanity as a whole.*[1]

If we take it seriously, culture is far from recreational, elitist or optional. It sits within the international rights agenda. It is an issue of justice, which plays out in pragmatic ways, as an essential service, like education, health. Culture is not benign. It is a powerful narrative contagion that binds us together.

Because of the power of culture, we need to pay attention to it, and be vigilant about everyone's rights, not for the few, or many, but for all. Because if we don't, it can be used against sections of society, demonising them or rendering their story invisible and citizenry vulnerable. We need to take the right to culture as seriously as other human rights, because insidious, slow genocides gain traction through the permissions that cultural invisibility can bestow on those on the fringes.

Therefore, we must keep an eye on culture—is it being trivialised? Does it have a persuasive seat in Cabinet? Is it sufficiently enshrined in legislation? Are government agencies such as the Australia Council for the Arts and other powerful bodies being good policy stewards of it? Is it for the few or for all?

Burnie is remote and on the fringe. Twenty-five years ago it gave rise to the organisation BIG *h*ART, the not for profit, campaigning arts company I work for, which bases its reason for being on the issues of cultural rights and cultural justice.

I accidentally discovered the north-west coast, straight out of home, the same year as that Midnight Oil song, and have felt the pull of place on my soul for almost two generations. Where I live has been Tommeginner country for 2,400 generations. This incredible cultural achievement by First Nations across the Australian archipelago is awe inspiring. But what does cultural continuity mean?

It is hard to grasp. Modern Australia is just ten generations old. Christ wore his crown of thorns a hundred generations ago. The 'ancient' Pyramids redefined the impossible 184 generations ago. Yet, these moments pale into insignificance compared to this eye-watering Aboriginal achievement of 2,400 generations. Governance, sustainability, ecology, secession planning—all managed orally—without a KPI or a business plan in sight. First Australians were applying ecological change management policies to help deal with the Ice Age 10,000 years ago ... How do we know? Because it is etched into rocks as petroglyphs on Murujuga (Burrup Peninsula) in WA, and this is almost modern history in terms of their timescale.

This culture, which Australia has worked so hard to deny, is very high culture indeed. It makes all those revered marble treasures of Western civilisation proudly encased in museum glass look a little naïve as we tout their importance in classrooms from Dubbo

High School to Oxford University. Our lauded ancient histories are mere Catherine-wheel civilisations spinning and spitting for a moment compared to the millennia of culture of this continent's Traditional Owners.

The fact that Tasmanian Aboriginal people like the Tommeginner have suffered a near-genocidal cultural trauma in the face of the tsunami of settler culture is not an accident, nor is it inevitable. It is the consequence of Aboriginal people being rendered invisible within a hegemonic culture by our newcomers' inaction and our blind eye, and thus devalued to the point when a genocide can be perpetrated.

This attempt at cultural genocide has slowed, but it has also shape-shifted, and we avoid the truth of our own complicity by blaming it all on the past and indulging in self-righteous, 'clicktivist' simplicities.

> *... the assumption that Western culture represents the best that has been said and thought implicitly devalues other cultures. In our post-imperial world, it is no more than a 'racially tinged absurdity.'*—John Carey, *What good are the arts?*[2]

In the West, we have claimed our (young) society's expressions of heritage and art as the highest form of culture, claimed it is *the* vital heritage globally. At the same time, we have enslaved future generations to 'the best' of our egotistical present and turned it into a heritage commodity.

We have to be careful here, not to hitch the right to culture to any one group or issue. It is a human right. We are all human—from the least privileged to the most. These rights relate to life itself.

> *Life is a luminous pause between two mysteries, which in the end are one.*—Carl Jung

The atomic building blocks of human beings were there from the big bang 13.8 billion years ago. Around 3.8 billion years ago there was life on earth, and the first humans arrived 200,000 years ago. Against this backdrop, well-fed human beings live for a small blip, a pause of a mere 720,000 hours.

Our moment of Jungian luminosity is a privileged chance at consciousness. An unlikely pause in which we can explore the self and unpack our momentary identity and experience, alongside that of others, our community, our society.

Culture could be described as the unfolding flow of our individual and communal attempts to make sense of this luminosity, collectively in the ephemeral present, before our 'luminous pause' recedes into the past.

As we work diligently at inventing and maintaining a past that no longer exists, and imagining a future, which is speculative, we forge our individual identity on the anvil of consciousness. This imagining, this collective act of hypnotic hypothesis, this selection of 'truths' from a potpourri of possibilities, propaganda and concocted canons is something called culture—and it is our best attempt at thriving, enriching the luminosity and stewarding a better/deeper world for the moment when we must pass on the baton.

Over millennia, this human right to culture has been hitched to many agenda. As we became separated into groups and tribes and nations, story-making became critically important as each built their own 'lived narrations', which keep people together and believing their narrations are the ones worth dying for. To embellish them we create artefacts, rituals, flags and symbols. These rituals are addictive, releasing our collective endorphins, and so we begin crafting yet more artefacts, ones that could be bought and sold. Artists, agents and connoisseurs saw a new kind of value in this, and what was once based on 'craft in everyday life', became elevated to a special category of high culture.

Until only about fifteen generations ago in the West, religion held a monopoly on these kinds of imaginative constructs to hold our existential despair at bay and reinforce the State, in a narrative alchemy of art, artefact, theology and cash. But then a few thinkers and patrons decided that religion didn't match up to the rigours of science and began chipping away with the pickaxe of logic.

In its place the arts, and the endorphins it releases, became the new idol, the new stairway to the sublime vacated by religion. What's more, the business model worked a treat: conveniently the 'high' arts could be bought and sold. You could buy your own little piece of the sublime. A salve from despair, rendered in oils or alabaster.

Art was now 'sublime', and great care was needed to prevent it being sullied by the 'ordinary craft' of the 'ordinary folk' from which it sprang. So while the more fortunate were groomed to consume this bread and wine, the rest were left with bread and circuses. It is, however, all part of the broad discussion of ideas, created and consumed collectively, in our momentary 'luminous pause', and we can call this culture.

This beloved cultural discussion is never in stasis. It is emergent. It is not an inanimate thing, but a continuous flow. It is collective and immersive. It has no keeper, no owner, no high or low, no set platform, and as our 720,000 luminous hours unfold we—as individuals or groups—are either visible within this narrative cultural flow, or we are adrift, pushed to the margins.

We may not see it easily at first, but the neglect of cultural rights can have a catastrophic effect in places like the north-west coast of Tasmania, Port Pirie, Roebourne, Bourke, or in invisible or indentured communities. What is frequently missed is the intrinsic value of these communities, the assets they can contribute, if we listen. The way they can resemble the canary in the coalmine warning us all of our future. Public policy failure inflicted, and the 'deep poverty' that flows from it, can act as a rich compost raising new approaches to serious community need.

Every one of us should have the right to participate, be represented in and consume their country's culture, to have a voice in the cultural discussion, to be visible in the narration; because it is our cultural right. But also because it is this discussion that will influence our collective future. To be invisible, to be shut out, creates a dangerous cultural twilight zone, in which it is very difficult to thrive.

Culture has this important protective function, and everyone has a right to that protection. Ask the Tommeginner people. Ask the kids playing on the sand in the Midnight Oil song 'Burnie'. Ask the talented, courageous and non-aligned arts organisations such as Back to Back Theatre, FORM, DADAA, Barkly Arts, Curious Works and many others in the under-represented, invisible and excluded communities delivering virtuosic practice against the odds. They know culture is not a plaything, a commodity, an add-on merely enhancing the lifestyles of those who can afford it. They know cultural inclusion is about safety. About the protection that cultural visibility can provide. They know it is not the funded luxury of an ascendant middle class, it is essential to all. And therefore it is urgent. We must be vigilant. And we must bring all the persuasive language of our passion for cultural justice to a harried legislature, and speak truth to power—not to bully them but to assist them to see the broad societal benefits of taking justice seriously.

1. Trial and Error

The purpose of theatre is not to fix the social fabric, not to incite the less perceptive to wake up and smell the coffee, not to preach to the converted about the delights (or the burdens) of a middle-class life. The Purpose of Theatre is to Inspire Cleansing Awe.— David Mamet.[3]

My home on the north-west coast of Tasmania has the cleanest air in the world, an incredible array of environments a short drive from home, the purest rain, the richest soil. It is the birthplace of permaculture, and the home of the Alexander Technique. And yet, viewed another way …

The electorate of Braddon (Burnie) is in the second percentile of social need in Australia. Over a third of residents depend on government allowances for their primary source of income. At last available figures, the median household income is $735 per week (the national median is $1,027). Twenty-eight per cent of children and young people in Wynyard are living in low-income households. The school retention rate for years 10 to 12 is only 47.6 per cent, compared to the state average of 60 per cent. Forty-nine per cent of Tasmanians aged 15–74 lack the basic literacy skills to cope with the demands of everyday life and work tasks in a knowledge-based economy, and Braddon is the worst. At Smithton High School, 40 per cent of Year 9 students scored below the minimum NAPLAN standard average. At Wynyard High 40 per cent of students who score above the minimum NAPLAN standard do not go through to complete Year 12.[4]

These statistics capture the daily struggle of many families to survive. One cause of their powerlessness is the invisibility of their communities which results in a policy collusion depriving them of the opportunity to change their social trajectory. This passive cultural abandonment results in an often accidental victimisation: the narrative blames the poor for poverty rather than poverty for people being poor. In other words, because many people don't have the access, literacy and opportunity that allow them to participate in positive representation, and have the nuances of their story recognised by the broader community, they are excluded from the mainstream. They are denied their cultural rights and lose the protection of inclusion.

Big *h*ART was set up in Burnie almost by accident: an opportunity for a small amount of project funding became available along with an invitation from the local council. A 'trial and error' attempt without much planning followed. Over 25 years, Big *h*ART has grown and become wedded to cultural rights: we make art and build communities to drive change among people who lack visibility. The change-making premise is simple—the work is motivated by the vital role of story as a social protector—captured in these few words: *'It's harder to hurt someone if you know their story.'*

Big *h*ART developed as a response to the changing economic and social conditions created by the closure of the paper mills in Burnie. The idea was to trial a non-welfare, task-focused approach to working with at-risk young people: assist them to learn the skills to tell their story within their own community and beyond, and in the process to learn new literacies, self-confidence and experience pathways to participation. This is well-illustrated by Darren Simpson, who participated as a fifteen-year-old in the early projects, *GIRL* and *Pandora Slams the Lid*, and whose life changed significantly:

> *I left school in Grade 9, so I didn't really get a good education. I just hung out with my mates doing whatever day to day life brought to us. My friend Nick Angel said one day that he was involved in the theatre project at the Burnie Civic Centre and suggested that I should go with him. I can remember that Nick and I had a corner we sat in so we could not really be noticed from the rest of the group.*
>
> *Scott was very good at getting the group and individuals doing a range of activities. It slowly brought us out of our comfort zone and built our confidence to stand up and talk about whatever the topic was, or what activity we would do.*
>
> *First, we did two shows; both nights were*

packed out, very nervous, with all our friends and family and people that supported the whole project. This was really big for us to do the show justice ... and we did. A very good group of people we all turned out to be, and we had a party up on the stage after the show. What a great feeling it was for me to stand up and perform in front of so many people.

After GIRL, *we did a show called* Pandora Slams the Lid, *and took the show around Tasmanian schools. We had grown a lot since* GIRL. *We were now roadies and performers.*

A couple of years later, in 1996, I got a job at Creative Paper Mill making handmade paper. The project was designed to help long-term unemployed people get a job by teaching us basic job skills making paper. I enjoyed making paper, it was different from normal jobs and very creative in the papers we made. When funding dried up, the business was opened to tourists to come in and see the process of how we made paper by hand.

I was given the role of Papermaker/Tour Guide. I love the fact I could now stand in front of people having all the attention on me as I explained the process, and being able to create different papers for artists to use out of recycled materials. I have done a huge amount of interviews, talking about

> *the paper I make, which has gone all around the world, including talking on NPC radio in the States. I have now been a worker here for 21 years and worked for the Burnie City Council, which I'm proud to be a part of, and have shown tens of thousands of tourists how I make paper, and I also have a Diploma in Travel and Tourism.*[5]

These young people, who (except for their street behaviour) were largely invisible to their community, were seen and valued in practical new ways, encouraging empathy and invitations to new futures from within community networks.

Setting our Principles

Our first group of participants ranged from withdrawn to volatile: from self-harming to harming the community. At the start there was one offence per week from the target group; at the conclusion of the first project we had one offence in ten months. This might make it sound like the work was highly organised and strategic. It wasn't. It had thought behind it, but in reality was a mad scramble to achieve something on almost no funding. Big *h*ART wasn't even an entity; it was a tenuously linked series of poorly funded projects.

However, the concepts behind it soon became clear. We were not to be a single issue charity, and we defined five foundational principles.

The Five Domains of Change

Individuals going through an issue had to be given new opportunities to make choices to change their social trajectory, and be supported through that process for at least a 150 weeks.

Communities needed the opportunity to understand these people in their midst, identify, observe and support the changes they were making, and develop as a community, building the foundations of a legacy for at least 150 weeks.

Nationally people in positions of power and policy needed to meet these individuals, hear their story, hear about the changes, and apply what they learned to policy development. In other words, to give them their cultural rights.

Art and content made with and in these communities had to represent the people and issues with the strongest possible aesthetic; be admitted into festivals and forums of influence. Virtuosity and aesthetic choices were to be critical to the power of those rights.

Knowledge and learning must then be passed on to others in the field to prolong the legacy of impact and better practice, and to ensure the wheel was not being perpetually reinvented.

By the time Big *h*ART officially became a charity in 1996, Tasmania was in the spotlight with a national tragedy—the Port Arthur massacre. Our response of anti-crime and anti-violence messaging proved a much-needed good news story for Prime Minister

John Howard, desperate for something Tasmanian and positive. So when we approached him to launch our charity in Canberra, he agreed, thus giving Big *h*ART good access to cabinet ministers for the next ten years.

The fact that we began in the marginal electorate of Braddon was important. The district is home to a muddle of ingrained and invisible issues driven by deep poverty, as people try and deal with the hand they've been dealt and the hand that keeps them down. *It is easy to neglect or damage people if you don't know their story.* We were fortunate to meet a wise retired lawyer in Burnie, who agreed to establish us as a registered charity, and he urged us to keep our structure as simple as possible. We were lucky also to be taught by this remarkable community. It turned out to be an entirely appropriate location for an arts company to experiment, be hothoused and begin to export projects nationally. We were learning how to fight for the cultural rights of those groups in the community that were marginalised.

In hindsight, the discoveries we made about 'culture as a right', pointed us towards 'culture as an essential service'—essential to assisting communities to thrive. This is illustrated well by *Lucky*, an intergenerational crime prevention and community development project on the north-west coast beginning in 2005 and concluding in 2009. (The following description of *Lucky* is a truncated version of a project evaluation by Peter Wright of Murdoch University.)[6]

The closure of Burnie's paper mill put many people out of work and the protests that surrounded it put many people out of work and brought on frustration and general disengagement. There were strong follow-on effects among the region's youth, with suicide, drug abuse, reckless and violent behaviour and teenage pregnancies all increasing. Big hART wanted to explore the notion that young people choose their pastimes according to the choices and opportunities they are given, and that an improved, vibrant living environment will ultimately alter adopted trajectories and result in a healthier community. It set up a base in a disused marine shed on the outskirts of Burnie Harbour and turned it into the Creative Living Centre, which became the major workshop space for the duration of the project. This new space provided a blank canvas for the young target groups to make their own, signalling a fresh beginning.

To engage with potential participants, Big hART teamed up with local service providers including Circular Head Aboriginal Corporation, No 13 Youth Centre, Community Corrections and Job Net Burnie, who directed Big hART staff towards young people whom they believed would benefit from participation in the project. Participants came equipped with an array of social and personal problems that had severely affected their self-esteem and had hindered their productive involvement in the community, at times leading them to poor choices and criminal or risky behaviours.

In the project's first stage, Big hART provided support for isolated young single mothers and their children by offering workshops in early childhood education in which the mothers were able to learn about all aspects of the healthy development of their children. In order to increase bonding and trust between the young mothers and their children Big hART took care to offer a wide variety of playful, fun activities that promoted close interaction between the families: toy-making, sculpture slams, creating family histories, painting, cartooning, print-making, dancing, lullaby writing and storytelling sessions. The art of play was at the centre of these activities, fostering the development of imagination and resilience in participants and preparing them to engage in widening social circles. Communication skills aiding professional development were additionally focused on in separate sessions including areas like public speaking, voice training and interviewing techniques. Jemma, one of the regularly participating mothers, testified

> *that this approach enabled participants to redefine their identities when she remarked to an outsider: 'They treated us like equals and looked past all that other "stuff" [that everyone else notices].'*

The mothers were given the opportunity to apply their new skills directly by joining Big *h*ART artists and other teenagers who were working on a spin-off project with shack communities across the north-west and west coasts of Tasmania called *Radio Holiday.* Linking the mothers in artistic practice with a social group that shared similar experiences of alienation on the outskirts of society quickly yielded a lively dialogue from which sprang a compelling array of oral history accounts that captured a way of life under threat from the changing use of the island's public lands. The mothers and other marginalised teenagers conducted interviews with 150 'shackies' from five communities and assisted Big *h*ART artists to create a series of live 'radio play' installations, which were presented at the Ten Days on the Island Festival in 2005.

Aside from the deepening connection between the young mothers and the 'shackies', *Radio Holiday/Drive-in Holiday* also provided social and professional engagement for other struggling teenagers. It greatly aided Bruce, a young man suffering from autism spectrum disorder and at odds with formal education settings, to discover in the arts a social space that was capable of accommodating his needs. In an intensive mentoring process, he sponged up knowledge about editing film and audio, as well as producing his own music, which he then performed as part of the project's team at the Melbourne International Festival of the Arts.

Big *h*ART took care to establish a broad base for the project's sustainable outcomes by setting up and maintaining strong networks with local governments, councils and service providers, inviting them into the project and keeping them up to date with the project's progression. This bond ensured that participants gained a positive profile not only with their immediate audiences, but also with local bodies and organisations, which in some cases led to employment opportunities for the teenagers.

The project successfully achieved its intention: to assist participants to give shape and voice to their own stories, to divert them from criminal trajectories, to develop new skills, to re-imagine alternative pathways and to (re)connect with each other and the community at large. This was reflected in the numbers: none of the constantly involved mothers re-offended, and 80 per cent of participants either joined the workforce or enrolled in further education, while many also joined other service-related groups and activities that aided in overcoming the isolation that had previously driven them.

A strong media strategy ensured that the project's reach exceeded its immediate audience and opened up possibilities for participants' continued evolution in the arts sector. At the same time it raised awareness of public issues like the changing nature of land use (*Radio Holiday/Drive-in Holiday*), the ageing population (*This is Living*) and the harmful behaviour to which some young men in remote areas were committing themselves (*Drive*).

This cluster of interlinked projects known as *Lucky* captures the five domains of change in Big *h*ART's approach working together. *Individuals* and their social trajectories; *communities* and responsive development; *national*—forays into policy and power; *content*—powerful and virtuosic story; and *knowledge* with others in the field. This approach to community arts and cultural development (CACD) had its foundation in decades of work by other companies in the sector. By trial and error, Big *h*ART sharpened its focus towards greater impact and began championing cultural rights across many platforms.

An urgency was developing in the work and a passion for a broader approach, beyond the self-limiting echo chamber of the arts, across government, business and community. Many of our results were highly sought-after across different portfolios because the evidence was strong. Communities can thrive if a more holistic and evidence-based commitment to cultural rights is supported.

> *Justice will not be served until those who are unaffected are as outraged as those who are.*—Benjamin Franklin

2. Making Art that is Big

> *When I saw the finished version of* Hipbone Sticking Out, *it hit me so powerfully that I was standing in tears, and I have never experienced that in my lifetime.*—Allery Sandy, Yindjibarndi elder from Roebourne, performer and grandmother to young Yijala Yala participants.[7]

There are many different terms used to describe the achievements of CACD workers—participatory process, intentional art making, community art etc. All of them value both content and process, rather than focusing on content alone. Content is one expression of creativity, and may at first appear to be the only commodity. However, the process of making the content, is also highly valuable across many sectors, and provides many doors to cultural participation. The process of making is not solely validated by the content outputs. There is validation in outcomes from deep engagement just as there is from the intrinsic and critically valued content created.

If delivered in the right way, this participatory process has a high dollar value across government, a point which is often missed by the creative industries. You only need to look at the 'Our Partners' page in the annual report of an organisation such as DADAA to see the breadth and depth of engagement of high-calibre CACD practitioners, and how much value they deliver across multiple policy areas.[8] We have a great opportunity for the sector to professionalise and partner across governments, portfolios, corporates and communities in much more sophisticated ways.

Like many other community arts and cultural development organisations, Big *h*ART works in remote, regional, isolated communities, with imprisoned, unhoused, elderly, young, at risk, disengaged collaborators. It is tough and rewarding work. The way we deal with issues of cultural justice shines a light on who we are as a country. As Martin Luther King said, 'Injustice anywhere is a threat to justice everywhere'. Participatory work equips outsiders and their communities to express themselves alongside professional artists, gain agency and empowerment, reclaim their cultural rights and contribute their voice in the 'narration that is the nation'.[9]

Communities are not bound by geography, they are complex cultural systems, of which geography is a part. What underpins the communities we work with is the organising curatorial principle of the invisibility faced by people driven to the outside: rural young people at risk of HIV through injecting drug use; teenage women with children at risk of family violence; young people witnessing extreme violence in regional areas; young men killing themselves in cars; immigrants drowning on

Australian beaches. These are interwoven with broader issues: Indigenous language loss; the legacy of nuclear testing on traditional lands; copyright ownership for the family of Albert Namatjira; isolation and fear in public housing and the need for safer communities.[10]

Choosing a Project

Big *h*ART receives many urgent requests to help address cultural rights issues in many communities. To decide whether to take on a project, we have to ask a series of questions: Is the issue being covered elsewhere? Are other platforms championing it better? Is this issue, or are the people experiencing it, invisible? Has the issue been abandoned by the 'change industry'? Who is making the request? From questions like these, plus the possibility of a constructive mutual learning relationship, by which both Big *h*ART and the community can learn from each other, a decision to initiate design thinking and pursue funding, is made.

For many outsiders, their story, and their quest for cultural rights is often the last remaining expression of agency they have. And these stories, if told with insight through working side by side with sensitive, highly skilled artists, can become a gift for their community, and the country as a whole. The content—shows, films, art-engagements—can create moments which audiences crave. Arresting authentic, intimate moments, grounded in place, which beckon audiences, the media, policy makers, and those in positions of influence, to listen and long for a more inclusive society. This is cultural rights in action.

Making content through large-scale, long-term, process-based projects in high-needs communities requires a certain kind of artist—one with an eye for both content and process. This dual focus is experienced as making art that is big—big in scale, in ambition and complexity. Big in meaning and in potential replication and value. It also requires big stamina. Big *h*ART has been fortunate to work with over three hundred exceptional artists over the years, from painters and filmmakers to actors and skateboarders. Lex Marinos describes his experiences and the brilliance of other artists he's worked alongside in the context of complex projects:

> *Twenty-five years ago, out of the blue, I received a call from Scott Rankin to see if we could meet to discuss a show working with a group of 'misfit' kids from Tasmania's north-west coast who'd found themselves on the edge of the juvenile justice system.*
>
> *I was at a career crossroads, having worked for a couple of decades in subsidised theatre with some radio and television, and then mainly in film and television. I wanted to do more theatre but was no longer in touch with the mainstream. It had moved on and so had I. I thought it uninteresting and outdated and it probably thought the same about me.*

Fortunately, Big hART *revitalised my love of theatre and its ability to affect change through powerful storytelling.*

However, Big hART *may not be every performer's cup of poison. Many, for perfectly legitimate reasons, don't want to work on new scripts, or with non-professional performers, or in remote areas. Many don't want to work with the political and the social and the bleeding-heart. Good luck to them. But, for others who enjoy these challenges, Big* hART *is a haven.*

Hundreds of brilliant artists have committed themselves and their art to many projects and performances over the years, and I've loved the opportunity to work with them, to laugh and cry and dream together. There are far too many to list here, but in mentioning a few I pay tribute to all. I think of Trevor Jamieson, mercurial actor/dancer/singer/storyteller at the centre of the indigenous trilogy: Ngapartji Ngapartji, Namatjira, Hipbone Sticking Out. *These were epic performances of wit, intellect and passion. Derik Lynch—with the angelic voice and wicked humour—joined Trevor in* Namatjira. *And the seemingly infinite permutations of women and kids from remote Indigenous communities who sang, danced and told stories alongside Trevor. I think of*

> *actors Glynn Nicholas and Leah Purcell, Kerry Walker and Kerry Armstrong; Simon Gleeson and Natalie O'Donnell, Sheridan Harbridge and Marty Crewes, Shareena Clanton and Jada Albert, Bruce Myles, Anne Grigg, Butoh-trained Yumi Umiumare, and many more.*[11]

As Lex captures, at their best, these projects feel so right. They are often cherished by artists, filmmakers, actors and animators as one of the deepest experiences of their career, full of meaning and a sense of coming home even though the settings can be volatile, and participation convoluted. High-needs communities are just that—high in need. Survival identity, low skills, low capacity and volatility can all contribute to community self-sabotage. There is never a perfect project and failure is always a critical part of the mix. Being a humble listener, rather than focusing on delivering 'solutions', is a vital skill for artists in these cultural rights settings.

The role of the producer is equally critical. Producers must be able to stand with artists as they engage with both process and content, building collaborative spaces, where creative integrity remains intact, as does the community. In other words, how to be virtuosic in both content and process. Artists may lean one way or the other but without this dual intentional excellence, the impact of projects on cultural rights will be small. Without virtuosic process, individual and community domains of change will be diminished. Virtuosic content, strong advocacy for marginalised communities—with media, specialist publics and political influencers—will remain meek. This tension is a key consideration when schooled and unschooled artists work together on cultural rights projects designed to drive powerful change.

Such projects are very hard to deliver. They can never be perfect. Failure and listening to failure will always be part of the process. Artists and producers who can live with the contradiction are rare. Big *h*ART has been privileged to work with over three hundred such professionals, many working with the company across decades. It is hard to glimpse the complexity of these layered projects and the big issues they tackle without experiencing them. If they weren't dealing with iterations of vexed issues involving sensitive cultural rights, they'd be simple to grasp. The following project descriptions try to capture that complexity and designed approaches across five domains of change.

NAMATJIRA (2009 to 2017)

> *The word is never said, but* Namatjira *is an enactment of reconciliation ... a sudden generosity of possibility. And that's a rare thing to witness ... a tribute to how artfully its makers step through the political minefield of this kind of community-based work.*—Alison Croggon, Theatre Notes.

From 2005 to 2008, Big *h*ART developed, with people from the Central Desert, a Pitjantjatjara language project called *Ngapartji Ngapartji*, which explored the aftermath of the British nuclear testing at Maralinga, and the theme of dispossession. One cast member was a fourteen-year old boy related to the painter Albert Namatjira. He was the quietest member of the cast and a beautiful artist who drew his country on stage throughout the performance. Each night at curtain, when he was introduced as Albert Namatjira's grandson, you could feel a ripple of recognition throughout the audience. As well as a deep affection for Namatjira, there was an unsettling feeling, a recognition of the injustice he and his family suffered. Night after night, we'd listen and wonder whether this compelling narrative could speak to the damaged heart of the country.

In 2009, the 50th anniversary of Albert Namatjira's passing, we began talking with the Namatjira family about their story and the need for recognition and justice. For twelve months we ran workshops in the community, exploring aspects of Namatjira's story and the family's aspirations. The first issue was the matter of copyright. Copyright in his work had been sold and the family earned almost nothing and benefitted in only very meagre and unjust ways.

So Big *h*ART's seven-year project began by partnering with Iltja Ntjarra Many Hands Art Centre in Alice Springs, and through this partnership, community workshops began in earnest in Ntaria (Hermannsburg) and Alice Springs to create a work for the stage. Belvoir

Street Theatre included the show in their subscription season and a strategy was devised to regain the copyright for the family. Exhibitions were assembled, in partnership with Iltja Ntjarra, to tour with the performance, and a feature-length documentary was commissioned.

The family wanted to tell their story and participate in the performance. Even though touring with a theatre show was a foreign experience, they came on tour and each night at intervals they drew in chalk on a huge backdrop, creating a compelling Namatjira landscape across the stage.

The Namatjira name was iconic, yet so many of the details of the narrative were not well known. At Belvoir, the show was immediately embraced and it sold out wherever it toured. In the theatre a sense of being witness to something special prevailed, as members of the family brought their country into the theatre. The combination of skills across the cast, which included virtuoso musician Genevieve Lacey, actor Trevor Jamieson, acclaimed portrait artists Robert Hannaford and Namatjira family artists, provided a rich mixture of cultures that touched the hearts of 50,000 audience members—with all earnings returning to fund the project.

Before and after the show, exhibitions of watercolours sold out, boosting art sales for the family. Painting workshops were held in towns and cities, with participants learning directly from the Namatjira family. School groups attended the production as awareness grew about the injustice with which the Namatjira family lived. People signed up to the 'Friends of Namatjira' campaign lending their support to securing the copyright. At the end of the tour the production returned to Ntaria where it was performed outdoors to hundreds of locals, who had driven across the desert to sit around fires and watch Namatjira's story unfold where it happened.

Building on the story of Albert's historic audience with a young Queen Elizabeth, and wanting to lift the profile of the copyright quest, the production toured to London, where it played at Southbank. The company was invited to Buckingham Palace to meet Queen Elizabeth, Prince Philip, Prince Charles and the Duchess of Cornwall. The Royals also met Albert's grandchildren, Kevin and Kumantjai L Namatjira Lankin, and the company. They discussed art and Alice Springs, and looked at the Namatjira paintings in the private collection. This all drew strong attention in the UK media to the copyright issue and helped build a groundswell in Australia.

Big *h*ART created a feature film documentary covering the project and its work to buy back the copyright. Rosemary Neill, writing for *The Australian*, and other journalists, picked up the issue, and in 2017 the philanthropist Dick Smith put up the funds to make the buyback a reality. Others assisted in setting up the Namatjira Trust with the family to help sustain the Hermannsburg art movement. And in August the Northern Territory Government reached a compensation settlement with the Namatjira family. This tightly focused project drove home these very specific cultural rights issues to achieve long-term change.

ACOUSTIC LIFE OF SHEDS (2015–)

> Acoustic Life of Sheds *sees power pop performed in a calving shed at Flowerdale, haunting experimental music fill a hay barn at Boat Harbour, opera ring out in an old stables and steel guitars bring a shearing shed to life at Table Cape.*—The *Mercury*, Hobart.

Acoustic Life of Sheds is a continuation of a decade's work creating site-specific projects in the Tasmanian hinterland, including *Lucky*, *Radio Holiday* and *Drive-in Holiday*, which, although exploring ephemeral landscape architecture and our changing relationship to rural heritage, are exploring much more—the invisible changes occurring in farming communities and the negative effect these have on communities.

Farming these small pieces of land has given rise to utilitarian sheds made from various repurposed materials from different eras, which dot the landscape. Many, abandoned or replaced by bigger sheds, still stand and carry histories and shadows of the past as they resist both technological change and the raging winds of the Roaring Forties that rattle their iron walls. In many ways, these communities have also been abandoned, cut adrift, leading to invisibility and a lack of services. Stand in these sheds and listen, and you'll feel an acoustic presence, but also a resonance of family and agricultural provenance, which is in danger of being lost.

The creative structure of *Acoustic Life of Sheds* is simple. Musicians spend months working with sheds across the landscape, collaborating with the shed architecture and farming families to harness sounds, stories and atmospheres, extending them to become part of the composition. The act of sitting down with a farming family and hearing the stories of who built the shed and how, creates an avenue for valuing this often hidden toil, and building connections back into the community.

During the performances, audiences drive between each shed over a 40km landscape, and discover each one transformed into a venue. Moving from property to property over an afternoon, they absorb each shed's acoustic life, the landscape, the music, the varied composition and the local produce. *Sheds* is a free event, years in the making, which gives rise to an unadorned atmosphere, story, slow conversation and virtuosity.

Below the surface, however, other issues are being explored: the highlighting of food provenance and sovereignty, the changing nature of farming, the loss and gain. Implicit questions arise and farming families and community networks connect. Although issues such as mental health are not directly addressed, they sit just below the surface and are felt in the patina of each shed and song. Most importantly, the project is plugged into the local high school, with each shed staffed by local young people, who have been beside arts professionals in community change-making, and who enjoy eye-opening new opportunities to overcome the barriers they often experience when seeking work.

Acoustic Life of Sheds is simple and pure in intention, examining the invisible life of farming families in the context of an arts festival. First performed for the 2015 Ten Days on the Island Festival in Tasmania, *Sheds* won the Art Music Award presented by APRA AMCOS and the Australian Music Centre for another selection of sheds in 2017, and has been invited again in 2019.

Acoustic Life of Sheds demonstrates a project prosecuting cultural rights, one which does not necessarily mean agitation or controversy. The language of each project needs to spring from the context, the diversity of the artists and the savvy of the producer.

PROJECT O (2014—)

> *I had the pleasure of seeing the work of the remarkable young women from Big* h*ART's* Project O, *who are taking positive action in rural communities affected by family violence. I am thrilled to see that this primary prevention project is now going national and promoting generational change.*—Rosie Batty[12]

Primary prevention is critical to long-term sustained change, and *Project O* is focusing on primary prevention by creating generational and attitudinal change to help de-normalise family violence. The project works with young women to increase their personal agency and build their skills through mentoring and community events. It successfully piloted in Tasmania, gained the attention of the Commonwealth Government Minister for Women, and has since been rolled out in Cooma, Canberra, Roebourne and Frankston North.

Project O gives rural young women the skills and confidence to drive change locally and in the digital space. It begins with peer-to-peer research and development workshops, through which young people identify the issues they are facing. This then develops into a skills workshop focused on girls aged 12 to 15, to increase their capabilities and strengthen their resolve to contribute to their community. As skills are gained, opportunities are created to use them in their community, building confidence based on real achievement, and changing negative attitudes to young women.

Central to *Project O* is an art endurance event, organised and run by the young women, known as *Colourathon*. The concept utilises street art on shipping containers, group colouring, digital art, music and publishing; and community groups work together alongside the young women to keep the art marathon going. Each hour is sponsored. It is a galvanising public event that brings the community together, raises the issue of family violence locally and provides a platform from which to lobby government and community power brokers in positive ways. An associated crowd-funding campaign also raises money to provide training in trauma therapy by the Australian Children's Foundation for the staff of government-funded family violence shelters caring for children fleeing violence. The last event, held in the sculpture garden at the National Gallery in Canberra, raised $40,000, with support from over a thousand people in communities around the country.

These brief project portraits have much in common, even though the issues they confront are varied. The layered approach sees participants contribute the gift of their story and they work alongside artists and arts workers to turn it into art. Through the art, they build visibility for the issues and visibility enables them to share their new-found leadership, shifts attitudes in their communities and affirms their cultural right to be included in the 'narration that creates the nation's future'.

To achieve this, Big *h*ART is fortunate to have a team of committed full-time collaborative producers and artists and a large pool of talented arts workers to call on for specific projects. Some of this core team have collaborated for almost twenty years, and other specialists return time and again to work on unusual projects about which they are passionate. The projects themselves are rarely less than three years in duration, and in complex communities can be up to eight years. They run simultaneously in a variety of locations, tackling diverse issues. In the beginning, Big *h*ART projects were almost voluntary. Now, however, the complexity and the potential risks in some communities have shaped the company into a unique structure: efficient, with almost no infrastructure, and which delivers high social value from a committed team.

Our practice

While some of these project portraits describe work with Aboriginal communities, Big *h*ART is not an Indigenous organisation. Indigenous people make and tell their stories through the valuable work of companies such as Yirra Yaakin, Ilbijeri, Blackfella Films, Bangarra and others. And we are sometimes invited to collaborate with Indigenous communities by clan elders, in places such as Roebourne in WA. These projects are processes of intercultural exchange and long-term collaborations guided by elders—and their advice and stewardship is essential to cultural protection, and for keeping project workers and participants culturally safe. Big *h*ART begins by listening and establishes an exit and legacy strategy from day one, so as to ensure skills are transferred and knowledge retained in the community. When we accept a request to work in an Aboriginal community, workers, artists, mentors and trainees work for similar wages, rather than within conventional fee structures. We also generally don't retain IP or copyright; and any royalties or box office takings go back into the work in communities.

It is not possible to detail the complexity of our projects and delivery, however here is a basic guide to making fewer mistakes on CACD projects:

Before starting out

- 'Do no harm' is a good starting point. Easier said than done.
- Ask and listen—be invited into a community by the community.
- Begin exit and legacy planning at the start.
- Think through gift and asset—what is strong and what is wrong.
- Avoid short-termism; ignore governments and electoral cycles.
- Avoid simplistic thinking; project funding encourages it, resist it.

The process

- Safety is central—personal, community and cultural safety.
- Projects need intergenerational influences; communities are layered systems.
- Projects need intercultural influences; communities are never homogenous.
- Avoid scarcity cultures and territorial approaches: form partnerships; but remember, some partnerships, like some meetings, are a waste of time.
- Seek collaborations: schooled artist alongside unschooled artist.
- Avoid CACD sectoral dogma but listen for experience.

- Projects must be multi-layered and designed across time.

Casting, text and performance

- All roles need to be mentoring roles so as to leave skills in the community.
- Commit to bringing in the best mentors, with the highest skills. The best is expensive, these communities deserve it.
- Audition an artist's values as well as their art.
- Language is important—'a person experiencing the effects of disadvantage', rather than 'a disadvantaged person' etc.
- Don't blame the poor for poverty; look for ways in which the system failed a person rather than how the person failed the system.
- At the beginning the work is 80 per cent process and 20 per cent content creation: 80 per cent doing and mentoring—these figures need to shift with growth.
- Invite the critics into the process, not just to view the finished content.
- Communities are never static—they are always changing. Look for the flow of positive change and grow it.

Churchill said, *'Success is never final and failure is never fatal'*. The most successful CACD project will always involve failure, heartache and regret—how we deal with failure is part of the process and the excellence.

3. To thrive or not to thrive? A question for funders.

What is at stake in culture—as it has always been though we frequently forget it—are the great questions of ultimate value: of how we can live together and what the quality of our collective experience should be. These have not disappeared in an age of cultural abundance. They are even more urgent, as the possibility of a truly human creative society is in one way more realisable, in another as far away as it has ever been.—Justin O'Connor[13]

Arts funding in Australia is a car crash. It's like being a passenger in an out-of-control Holden about to hit black ice on the road from Cradle Mountain, while the driver posts a filtered lifestyle selfie on Insta capturing the serenity. But you're not allowed to say anything sensible, like, 'watch the road' apparently.

Four wonderful words: community, art, cultural, development. There are times when a career in CACD doesn't feel like a job at all. It can be playful and full of meaning; even when the hours are long and the pay short, it can feel like a privilege. Career paths in CACD are only nominally there. Mostly, you make your own way. Many CACD artists don't really know how they 'got here'. The sector can feel like that because it is a 'whole of life' experience; it is the way communities are. They are always developing; art is always being made at the grassroots. Participatory activities have always been the foundation of art, as part of everyday life. But then, somewhere in the midst of modernity, through value recognition, the instrumental value of the arts was formalised alongside the intrinsic value, and the battle lines were drawn—only to diminish the whole.

The Australian Council for the Arts was established in 1968 and became the Australia Council for the Arts in 1973. The Whitlam Labor Government, advocating for the rights of ordinary people to participate in the arts, instituted the Australia Council's Community Arts Program as a means of encouraging ordinary people's engagement in culture and supporting creative expressions of Australian national identity. The Australia Council wanted to ensure a sustainable future for the existing performing arts status quo, but then the establishment of the Crafts, Aboriginal Arts and Community Arts boards allowed for applications from artists to work in communities, which was a direct challenge to the old order and one that extended beyond its definition of art into government's social responsibility for preserving traditional practice, cultural continuity and community good. As outlined by Katharine Brisbane, in 1986 a report commissioned by the Federal Government's expenditure committee recommended that Commonwealth arts support policy should aim to democratise culture by ensuring wide and steady community access to a diversity of cultural experiences. This plan included putting a Community Cultural Development Unit between the councillors and the five boards through which to filter applications. 'By this time, of course, the now-established arts sector was all on the side of high art and saw democracy as a threat to their share of funding.'[14]

The Community Arts Board was converted to the Community Cultural Development Committee (CCDC) in July 1987, in the wake of radical welfare rhetoric that continued to underpin community arts policy.[15] Community arts have always been the problem child banging the leftist drum. In response, reformers have often wanted to 'leave it to local government'. However, those of us practising in the sector are also in part responsible for this marginalisation, through unhelpful, self-imposed dogma and categorising, the lack of professional development, limited creativity in generating income or finding funding, territorial insecurity, a fear of criticism and a scarcity culture.

Within this struggle, there have been decades of truly remarkable, dedicated and important work in the field, and as DADAA pointed out to the 2015 Senate Inquiry into the impact of the 2014 and 2015 Federal Budget decisions on the arts:

> *The community arts and cultural development sector has been incredibly effective at building sustained partnerships around complex Australian communities.* [16]

And that now, 40 years of CACD practice in Australia is at serious risk. However, although this is true, it has always been at risk, sometimes at the hand of clumsy policy and sometimes by our own hand in the sector. It is a serious issue, because cultural rights are put at risk.

CACD history is not to be taken lightly. What government chooses to do or not to do in relation to government spending on culture reflects value choices that are politically determined, and these choices will produce discernible societal outcomes. Public funding of culture can reproduce the social hierarchy by preserving, or even strengthening, inequality between social groups: Tal Feder and Tally Katz-Gerro suggest:

> *The use of art to exert power is twofold. On one hand, the privileged group tries to secure the hegemonic status of its culture as superior and legitimate and to establish a consensus on what constitutes cultural capital in the field. On the other hand, once this consensus has been established, this group seeks to limit access to certain cultural arenas within the larger field of art. Limited access to these areas allows members in the privileged group to express their dominant status by participating*

> *in the consumption of art and by accumulating the cultural capital that is associated with the consumption of legitimate art.*[17]

And in the Australian context, Justin O'Connor says it better than I:

> *The rationale for arts funding has been reduced to a bare stump of 'excellence' and the remit of the ABC to the politicians' cry for 'balance'. However, the real problem lies in the erosion of a shared language of public value, one that has had a more direct impact on culture than on almost anything else.*[18]

And, as artists like The Preatures' vocalist Isabella Manfredi know, 'You can't have excellence at the top of any field without a grassroots community'.[19] 'Arts ministers and government budgets create an atmosphere in which the arts can flourish or die', says Tamara Winikoff (then executive director of the National Association for the Visual Arts). 'All the experimentation, all the exploratory work takes place at a small-to-medium level, and yet its importance is not so well recognised, particularly by Coalition governments.'[20]

Stat-chat: CACD funding 2016–2017[21]

- 28 Major Performing Arts Board (MPAs) received 62 per cent of Australia Council Funding, totalling $109.1m, an average of $3.9m per MPA.
- 590 small-to-medium sized organisations shared funding of $54.3m, an average of $90,508 per organisation for the year.

While the MPA organisations received $109.1m:

- The CACD sector shared $6.1m (9 per cent of grants and initiatives funding);
- The Aboriginal and Torres Strait Islander sector received $5.3m (8 per cent of grants and initatives funding).
- Support for innovation was minimal, with $2.4m (4 per cent of the budget) going to Emerging and Experimental Arts.
- Artists with a disability received $1.3m (there are 4.3 million people in Australia with a disability,[22] and 8 per cent of artists in Australia identify as having a disability).[23]
- The number of artists working in the CACD sector has decreased from 3,000 in 1993 to 1,200 in 2016.

The small-to-medium sector is where most activity occurs in the cultural equity and access space. However, there is no pathway for a successful CACD organisation to take across from the sector to the MPA funding. This virtually abandons CACD practice to small-scale impact and mediocre outcomes.

And this is the nub of the problem. It is not that there is no money, it is a question of priorities. Arts agencies are pretending that their priorities are addressing these issues of disadvantage and cultural rights, but they are just not funding it. The majors have priority and everything else is minor.

It may sound like CACD artists just having a whinge, but these issues are on the minds of many in Australia's arts community and are even on the radar of the *New York Times*. In an article published on 2 September this year, Yaron Lifschitz, artistic director of Brisbane-based circus company Circa, declared that the Australian Government was entrenching a culture in our performing arts of 'overfunding mediocrity' and that many of the majors were 'arteriosclerotic—playing heritage works to aging audiences'. In the same article, Wesley Enoch, director of the Sydney Festival, commented wryly: 'We can sometimes have a very narrow bandwidth for cultural expression' and that funding should go to a broader range of companies to allow groups to 'explore new and interesting stories'.[24]

The MPA (framework) had fine ambitions, but the time is up for this kind of funding. With the exception of a handful of majors who expand and deepen our cultural landscape, these companies are sozzled from a heady cocktail of mediocrity, heritage and laziness. They sit in the middle of metropolitan centres, pandering to a constituency who don't need to be subsidised, and ignoring the cultural issues and the deprived communities in need of such skills and resources.

The question has to be asked: major in what? Scale maybe, but not in importance. Major in significant contribution to the nation? Major contributors to innovation? Major in support of up and coming artists? Major in addressing issues of access and equality? Major in cultural contribution to our region? Or in support of the art and culture of First Nations people? Major in reflecting cultural diversity in our community? Or perhaps just major in terms of size? As suggested by Jo Caust in *The Conversation*:

> *There has been a view that 'excellence' is a code word for large and important rather than excellent in terms of the quality of the work. Major organisations by their nature are seen as excellent whereas medium and smaller organisations are not.*[25]

This is not an either/or proposition. The MPAs deserve funding provided they innovate and put cultural justice front and centre in their practice. If they reflect the diversity of the community in content, and seek treatment for their European heritage addiction, fund them. Fund them to share their halls, resources and IP with prisoners and refugees, and fund them to deliver their main program in regional centres. Justice, equity, inventiveness, creativity, reach, scale, process, accessibility—these things need to sit alongside virtuosity and the occasional piece of heavenly heritage.

Put their work for children front and centre, along with hospice work and Indigenous communities (and not once in a while—make it their core business). This is an issue of human rights enshrined internationally. If they can't live up to what is required of them in a decent society, defund them.

In the current arts ecology, these institutions are never really challenged by the real world—through lazy peak-body leadership, they have become untouchable, unanswerable. MPA funding allows them to employ small teams of fundraising professionals to trawl for sponsorship and philanthropic funds through every sector of society. They are like mega-trawlers scouring the funding ocean and leaving nothing for those smaller companies who can't afford funding departments yet are doing the hard yards in terms of equity, access, justice and artist development.

Some of these major companies are good at filling hotel beds for large global businesses by dragging people to the cities for the occasional blockbuster, but they should be funded through events or tourism portfolios. Using precious arts dollars to fund this kind of cultural candy is like using health dollars to fund obesity.

Another less known reality is that they're not even reaching half as many people as the small-to-medium companies. Ben Eltham has done some excellent reporting on this.[26] In 2014–15, small-to-medium companies had a combined audience of 6.87 million people, while

MPA companies reached 3.37 million, less than half as many. The disparity in funding reveals the scale of the mismatch. In 2014–15, MPA companies were to have received $106 million in funding, and small-to-medium companies just $23.1 million.[27] The funding data makes it possible to calculate the relative subsidy per audience member for the two different types of arts organisations. Major companies collectively receive a subsidy of $31.50 per audience member. Small-to-medium companies receive a quarter of the funding, but deliver twice as many bums on seats: a subsidy of $3.36 per audience member. In other words, major companies get a whopping nine times the subsidy of the small-to-medium companies.

I suppose the MPA companies are just responding to twenty years of policy settings. The Australia Council's strategic plan declares: 'We will adapt the way we invest in the arts to increase our impact and become more open and reflective of evolving arts practice.' Really? The MPA structure is driven by ideas and policy designed in a different century, a pre-digital world. Before mass terrorism, before climate change, before native title, before the GFC, before the widening wealth gap. The world is a different place now and the issues more urgent, yet arts funding remains essentially the same. Cultural policy must be rebuilt from the ground up to meet the urgencies of the twenty-first century. We need to stop encouraging debilitating clusters of cultural sameness, while robbing high-needs communities of their human right to culture. Robbery is what it is.

Few people want these heritage companies to disappear, but we must free up funding for what really counts. We need to support the hotbeds of innovation: those that venture to dangerous corners of the community; those that create without wasteful infrastructure; companies focused beyond the intrinsic and instrumental value. And bring them together. Those who make only new work, experiment in new forms and new settings. Innovative nuanced new Australian work. Wonderful failures. Remote places. Brilliant attempts with outsider communities. Companies pursuing cultural rights.

The Australia Council publically declares that their priority areas are Aboriginal and Torres Strait Islander people, youth, regional and remote, people living with a disability; but the way they fund implies the opposite. The least amount of funding to the highest areas of need, and the companies which receive the highest levels of funding do the least in these priority areas. For all their rhetoric, the Australia Council does not have the resources to meet their commitment to high-needs communities: it does not have the funding capacity to match their ambition to reach the priority group in their strategic plan, nor for scalable and responsive funding or policy. The Australia Council is dabbling in this vital area of CACD, and the consequences are profound.

For the small-to-medium sector, applying for multi-year or project-based funding, their capped funding of $100,000 disadvantages the more successful organisations who are delivering more, with more excellence, at more expense. If you are turning over $200,000 a year and you get a $100,000 grant, you are in clover. If you are turning over $250,000 a month and get a $100,000 grant because that is all you are allowed to apply for, you are in tears. It is a question of need and scale. It makes more sense to stay small.

A decade ago Big *h*ART handed back what was considered a sizeable grant to the Australia Council, because their slicing and dicing of funding endangered the safety of our arts-workers in the field. It took courage to stand up to our peak body, and it caused damage to our reputation. We did it because we have a duty of care. Small-to-medium companies working in priority areas are forced to compete for funding, to reduce their budgets and increase their deliverables so as to 'win' funding. This sets up a practice of exploiting arts-workers by underfunding projects. The more you promise to do in these higher risk priority areas, the more likely you are to be funded. And the more likely to end in burnout. Our arts ministers need to be mindful of these duty-of-care issues, which flow from a focus on high-need cohorts combined with unreliable funding. Our culture is a human right; we should back it with the language of a right and fund it like a right.

But instead, we've got a car crash …

> *Keep your eyes on the road and your hands upon the wheel.*—The Doors

4. The potential power of cultural rights

> *I want to see a country where the arts flourish and breathe life into, well, everyday life. I want to see a country where the arts are available to us all and help us express ourselves as unique individuals, brought together in diverse communities. I believe the arts and creativity are integral and inseparable parts of what it is to be human. It concerns me that a mindset still persists in which only those things that can be counted matter, and things not easily quantified are too quickly discarded. Using that mindset, some argue the arts are simply a nice thing to have. I wholeheartedly disagree.*[28]—Jacinda Ardhern, New Zealand Prime Minister

These are the reverberating words of a strong prime minister who understands that culture is a fundamental right, not a luxury. This is a prime minister who advocates for the critical importance of cultural rights from the pinnacle of government. Come on Aussie, come on, come on—we can do better.

In government terms, CACD practice could sit in a strategic place across many portfolios, offering the taxpayer real value for money. The methods, disciplines and crafts it employs enhance what it means to be human. CACD is evidence-based and relevant to many of Government's most urgent objectives and essential services: health, education, justice, community safety, environmental sustainability, social harmony. The CACD sector should be powerful, sought-after and well-funded, but in fact, the opposite is true. It sits at the bottom of the arts barrel, drip-funded through a gauze of sympathy and a tinge of guilt.

By way of example, Big *h*ART has not survived for 26 years on cultural funding (less than 9 per cent of turnover), it has survived on a whole range of funding options from many different portfolios across governments that are 'open for business', because they need to buy what the CACD has to offer. The value of the work hasn't changed, but the way it is framed has: culture as a whole-of-life, whole-of-government proposition.

Safer communities, less violence, fewer prison sentences, less recidivism, longer life, less addiction, better engagement in education, economic development, stronger tourism, less slavery, fewer road accidents, decreased community and lateral trauma, and on the other side better cultural diplomacy, cleaner supply chain, more community development, decreased addiction, decreased depression and more bums on seats in the arts. These are valuable to government and society and can be driven by the work of CACD.

The social value of this CACD work is well recognised by some developers and global companies, the mineral resources sector and some areas of government. While the not-for-profit CACD sector has been hiding its light under a bushel, mesmerised by Australia Council 'petty cash', a commercial 'community development' industry has sprung up around the country offering limited parts of CACD practice to developers and government, at a higher premium. They are not connected to the sector and are not hindered by community arts dogma and fragile agendas. However, their practice is often limited, event-focused, solution-based, limited in local consultation and short-term.

It is the deep community dramaturgies that are missing, that underpin cultural rights and are the stock-in-trade of the very best of CACD practice—the inventiveness, close listening and integrity of thoughtful narrative practice. What is missing is the commitment of artists such as Bruce Gladwin at Back to Back Theatre or Lynda Dorrington at FORM—both intelligent values-driven artists combining aspects of CACD practice with other nuanced practice to achieve powerful important work. As a sector, we have let this happen by not valuing our work and making the arguments for it across government and other stakeholders. We've allowed ourselves to be dictated by timid arts agencies and have placed a low financial value on CACD practice in high-needs communities. As a consequence, we often don't see the value to government of CACD practice and don't insist on decent levels of funding.

Compounding this, there is limited training in CACD, no real support for career paths and negligible ongoing professional development. Peak bodies such as the Australia Council have failed to match with sectoral support the urgencies and complexities of twenty-first century communities. As the needs increase, we've been left standing and essentially de-skilling. Digital justice is now one of the most critical issues of our time, and what are we doing about it?

It's a global, digital world. The nature of work is transforming. The jobs of the future are unknown. Suddenly, knowing how to think, rather than what to think, is critical. What better place to learn the 'how' of thinking than in the arts? Failure is the compost for innovation. Right brain rather than left brain is an asset. As a basis for today's education add the A for arts to STEM (science, technology, English, mathematics) and you get STEAM.

The cultural sector has the opportunity to place itself at the centre of education, and CACD offers a humane approach where cultural rights, social value and economic value are aligned.

This underlying 'whole of life' language has much in common with that of First Nations people, who often have no exclusive word for art, because in their culture there is no separation between art and life, between country and your heart. The high culture of Aboriginal Australia, matured over millennia, is calling us to a better practice. A unique contemporary practice, forged by place, a practice we could share.

Long-term, intercultural projects such as *Ngapartji Ngapartji* and *Namatjira* taught Big *h*ART this holistic approach as a company, and it is what we are learning now through our work in Roebourne in the Pilbara. Perhaps the country is calling us back to a less fractured approach to art in the twenty-first century, one where cultural rights sit at the centre, returning us to a whole-of-life perspective—and, consequently, the whole of government as a funding pool.

The Way Forward

What will the cultural sector look like in 2050, when Australia is a modern Asian country? Here we are, a small population of 25 million, steadfastly clinging to the cultural traditions of nineteenth century Eurocentric heritage, all while one of the most profound transformations in human history is unfolding on our doorstep: Asian countries are constructing a powerful middle class of discerning and enthusiastic art consumers.

Just across the water is the country with the largest Muslim population in the world. Yet, instead of collaborating, Australia still sees itself as distant. Right now, if you take the over-70 population of India and China, you have a population the equivalent of the fourth largest nation on Earth. This group will soon be cashed up, experience-hungry grey nomads. Yet from our cultural ministers, agencies and peak bodies there is little in the way of 'welcome', or information sharing, just timidity and radio silence instead of opening a cultural conversation with sensitivity.

Uluru currently receives about 275,000 visitors a year. This is set to rise dramatically. Traditional owners such as Sammy Wilson are generous and welcoming, but where is the cultural planning and support for remote communities who will soon be welcoming growing numbers of visitors with almost no knowledge of Indigenous cultural life? Where is the cultural awareness to underpin it? There are so many opportunities for our cultural sector to support Aboriginal Australia, and for fragile regional or rural communities to embrace this incredible potential.

We must stop framing culture as 'just the arts' and start framing our work as having an impact on the 'whole of life', and as urgent and relevant to every part of the social policy spend. Culture, and therefore cultural rights, are not the gravy on the economic meat and potatoes. Culture is nutrition itself.

But embracing this does not mean we diminish the opportunities for finessed, highly specialised creative endeavour; instead we enhance it by opening up more opportunities to embrace diversity and inclusion in the process of making art and in its outcome.

> *It is not expected that every project the Commission funds or undertakes will serve the entire public, nor must every grant or project deliver broad and general public value. Some projects are narrow, deep and*

> *specific; some don't focus on a public event, but make possible the creation of work that adds to the artistic canon. These are no more or less valuable than those that serve a large number of people.*[29]

This is the view of twenty-first century practice in Arizona. It delivers engagement, builds participation and develops audiences, not by tricking the public just to get bums on seats, but because 'life'—our Jungian 'luminous pause'—is of exquisite value, and reflects the mysterious way in which the universe is, as it has been for billions of years, playing cat and mouse with entropy.

Our cultural right is the right to thrive—to live deeply, luminously, through a whole life, a creative life. Because of this whole, our individual 720,000 hours can be a creative manifestation of the pure joy of the universe. This creative hunger sits within the very best CACD practice—to activate, not pacify—and it can be felt and experienced in many ways: the singing of a Ngarluma tjaabi in the Pilbara at dawn; the confidence of an at-risk young person speaking proudly in public for the first time; simple Brahms played exquisitely; deep silence in a theatre as an actor disappears shaman-like; a moment when a parliamentarian experiences connection through story and finds the courage to speak out for justice. None of it should be wedded to the self-limiting debate as to whether the value of the arts is intrinsic or instrumental. Culture is broader, it gives meaning to the whole of life.

So how do we get there? Julianne Schultz suggests a new way forward:

> *Australia became a signatory to the UNESCO Convention on Cultural Diversity a decade ago, but the import of this has also not been exercised or realised. This provides a legal rationale for a reorganisation. The starting point is to put all cultural activities into a single portfolio, or one linked by clear lines of accountability. By comparison, in most comparable countries culture has been aggregated into one portfolio [. . .] recognis[ing] that if this sector is to achieve its potential for citizens, companies and the national interest, it needs to be taken seriously and that government needs to work on ways to enable a sustainable, innovative and profitable sector.*[30]

If this is true then we must fight passionately for it, with the powerful language of the law. We must amplify CACD practice. We must combine its core values with other genres and virtuosities to subvert mediocrity. We must offer up a powerful community dramaturgy that can 'enhance and advance' cultural rights and by doing so contribute to a more equitable society.

All our voices are needed for this contribution—First Nations people, statisticians, the wise elderly, writers, historians, refugees, academics, DJs, dancers, scientists, politicians, people living with a disability, media, diverse communities, inventors, perceptive young people, teachers—must show leadership and ensure *all* stories can be included, not just the active, articulate and privileged, because everyone, everywhere has the right to thrive. You cannot thrive if you are written out of your nation's ongoing narration. If you are not included, you will become invisible, and you will be easily damaged and hurt by your own country. And hurt turns into anger. And anger makes our communities less safe. And so the cycle continues …

In the end it is relatively simple. Cultural rights are a human right—for everyone—not for one group. Not the privileged nor the powerful. Not exclusively for First Nations and not just the excluded. For all of us. Because it is a question of justice, we must use the language of justice. And we must not be swayed. We must argue with the persuasive force of international law, even if these rights remain in part aspirational. We must bring the mature passion of a national leader such as Noel Pearson to bear on the political timidity of those in peak cultural bodies who are easily deflected from grasping opportunity.

We do not have the luxury of just tweaking the edges of cultural policy. We must get the centrality of the issue sorted. Culture is a human right, the right of all to be seen and heard in our nation's narrative, the right to be safe. Every time a cultural body like the Australia Council gets the policy settings and the funding wrong, they are robbing the most vulnerable in the community of their protection.

If culture is a right, the way we generate cultural policy has to change. The boards of the MPAs will have some serious questions to answer. Corporate sponsors will need to look closely at the way they spend their shareholder dollar. If culture is a right, the way we train our students will have to change. The central issue is broader than excellence in art, it is also about excellence in justice. The question that needs to be asked by cultural institutions is, 'Are we part of the problem?' Are we—with the best will in the world—doing harm to those who need our help the most?

Cultural funding has lost its way. But this cannot divert us in the field. We have to keep pushing, calling it out. We have to help culture earn a place of power at the cabinet table. Here's Jacinda Ardhern again:

> *In changing the way we make decisions, we can start addressing other issues too. One of those is universal access to the arts. For this to happen we need to gain a clearer picture of the reach of the cultural sector across New Zealand. With that information we can develop policies that ensure our investment in the arts and culture reaches everyone. It will also mean ensuring the diversity of our communities is represented in the governance and leadership of our cultural sector. We won't see the arts available to all if the voices of younger people, Māori, Pasifika and women aren't heard.*[31]

Perhaps this prime ministerial wisdom is made possible because New Zealand has had a treaty on which to build a human rights agenda. Perhaps a treaty as a powerful foundational chapter in the 'narration that is the nation' has given rise to an openness and hunger for visibility, inclusion, cultural justice and safety. Perhaps that points a way for Australia—a way in which our cultural peak bodies could lead us.

We have had strong leadership before in this cultural domain. In 1992, in his Redfern speech, Prime Minister Paul Keating began by describing the Mabo decision:

> *By doing away with the bizarre conceit that this continent had no owners prior to the settlement of Europeans, Mabo establishes a fundamental truth and lays the basis for justice.*

He then went on to challenge the nation to 'imagine', to see a story that was invisible to the majority:

> *It might help us if we non-Aboriginal Australians imagined ourselves dispossessed of land we had lived on for 50 thousand years—and then imagined ourselves told that it had never been ours.*
>
> *Imagine if ours was the oldest culture in the world and we were told that it was worthless.*
>
> *Imagine if we had resisted this settlement,*

> *suffered and died in the defence of our land, and then were told in history books that we had given up without a fight.*
>
> *Imagine if non-Aboriginal Australians had served their country in peace and war and were then ignored in history books.*
>
> *Imagine if our feats on sporting fields had inspired admiration and patriotism and yet did nothing to diminish prejudice.*
>
> *Imagine if our spiritual life was denied and ridiculed.*
>
> *Imagine if we had suffered the injustice and then were blamed for it.*
>
> *It seems to me that if we can imagine the injustice we can imagine its opposite. And we can have justice.*

Our country's leader implored us to imagine—it seems a far-off land now, such eloquence. What Keating was invoking is a powerful mechanism for change, imagining a different future. In so doing, the highest office in the land was championing the power of cultural rights. He was suggesting that a vulnerable group in society could be protected by the majority, through our collective reimagining. The legislation of Mabo was vital, but legislation is the stick, whereas culture—our collective re-imagining, re-telling to earn permission to re-make—is the carrot. To be effective, legislation needs the powerful permission of our collective reimagining. All citizens deserve the right to be visible within this constant reimagining, this narration that creates our constantly emerging nation. This is about cultural justice. And it requires our vigilance. It requires our passionate persuasive powers as artists and communicators, asserted with the language of the law, that cultural rights are not some add-on, or some creative instrument to drive languishing sections of the economy; or a recreational middle-class luxury, or some tool for preservation of victor-histories. This essential human right has an agreed international imprimatur, a serious authority, which requires a senior ministerial seat at the table of government.

Endnotes

1 Alesia Koush, 'Right to Culture: Value Education for Culture, Peace and Human Development'. *Journal of Art Crime:* Spring 2017, p. 59–71. http://www.artcrimeresearch.org/journal-of-art-crime/

2 John Carey, *What good are the Arts?* Faber, 2005.

3 David Mamet, *Three Uses of the Knife*, Columbia University Press, 1998.

4 Sources: Australian Bureau of Statistics SIEFA Social Index; Tasmanian Council of Social Services Reports; Tasmania Police Corporate Performance Annual Report; 2014 NAPLAN Results; My School Data KCF Outcomes Framework Regional Profile.

5 *Big* h*ART, 25 Years Vol 1: Projects.Places.People.* Big *h*ART, 2017.

6 *Big* h*ART, 25 Years Vol 2: Essays.Research.Ideas.* Big *h*ART, 2017.

7 *Big* h*ART, 25 Years Vol 1: Projects.Places.People.* Big *h*ART, 2017.

8 http://www.dadaa.org.au/wp-content/uploads/2017/01DADAA-Annual-Report-2017.pdf

9 Edward W. Said, *Culture and Imperialism*, Vintage Books, 1994.

10 The projects referred to here are: *Pandora Slams the Lid*, *Inkwings*, *Scissors Paper Rock Cereal*, *Drive*, *Happy Water Sad Water*, *Ngapartji Ngapartji*, *Namatjira Project* and *Stickybricks*.

11 *Big* h*ART, 25 Years Vol 1: Projects.Places.People.* Big *h*ART, 2017.

12 Rosemary (Rosie) Batty became a domestic violence campaigner following the death of her eleven-year-old son Luke, who was murdered by his father. In 2015 she was voted Australian of the Year.

13 Justin O'Connor, *After the Creative Industries: Why we need a cultural economy*, PP47, May 2016.

14 Katharine Brisbane, *The Arts and the Common Good*, PP43, May 2015, pp. 30–31.

15 Kate MacNeill, Jenny Lye, Paul Caulfield, 'Politics, reviews and support for the arts: An analysis of government expenditures on the arts in Australia from 1967 to 2009', *Australian Review of Public Affairs, Vol 13,* 2003.

16 DADAA Ltd. is a key disability/mental health and community arts organisation for Western Australia that regularly offers programs in regional areas. The acronym stands for Disability in the Arts, Disadvantage in the Arts, Australia.

17 Tal Feder and Tally Katz-Gerro, 'Who benefits from public funding of the performing arts? Comparing the art provision and the hegemony-distinction approaches.' *Poetics 40*, pp 359–81, 2012.

18 Justin O'Connor, *After the Creative Industries: Why we need a cultural economy*, PP47, May 2016.
19 Isabella Manfredi, 'It's Become an International Joke': Isabella Manfredi Speaks At NSW Music Hearing', https://themusic.com.au/.../it-s-become-an-international-joke-isabella-manfredi-speaks...
20 Steve Dow, 'State of the Arts: How the Abbott Government is funding a high-culture war', *The Monthly*, October 2014.
21 Australia Council for the Arts 2016–17 Annual Report.
22 Australian Bureau of Statistics, Disability, Ageing and Carers, Australia: Summary of Findings, 2015.
23 Australia Council for the Arts 2017-18 Annual Report.
24 Clarissa Sebag-Montefiore, 'Is the Way Australia Funds the Arts a Recipe for Mediocrity?', *New York Times*, 2 September 2018. https://www.nytimes.com/2018/09/02/arts/australia-performing-arts-funding.html
25 Jo Caust, 'A budget to rebuild trust—but not trust in the Australia Council', *The Conversation*, 13 May, 2015 https://theconversation.com/a-budget-to-rebuild-trust-but-not-trust-in-the-australia-council-41750
26 Ben Eltham, *Crikey* https://www.crikey.com.au/2015/09/18/brandis-is-wrong-small-arts-orgs-deliver-much-greater-bang-for-govt-buck/
27 According to the Australia Council's submission to the Senate inquiry into Arts Minister George

Brandis' diversion of a third of arts funding to his Ministry in 2015.

28 Jacinda Ardhern, Opinion piece for ABC RN's *Big Ideas* series 3 September 2018. https://www.thebig idea.nz/stories/soapbox-opinion-piece-by-janda-adern

29 Arizona Commission for the Arts, *Creating Public Value*, Phoenix, 2004.

30 Julianne Schultz. 'Cultural economy and the soft power of the forgotten portfolio', *The Mandarin*, 1 June 2015. https://www.themandarin.com.au/ 35492-julianne-schultz-culture-arts-economy/

31 Jacinda Ardhern, Opinion piece for ABC RN's *Big Ideas* series 3 September 2018. https://www.thebig idea.nz/stories/soapbox-opinion-piece-by-janda-adern

Appendix:
Big *h*ART performances list

1992—1994
Girl (theatre)
Youth crime prevention project–Burnie, Tasmania
Pandora Slams the Lid (theatre)
HIV awareness project—Burnie, Tasmania
Girl and Pandora Slams the Lid (tour)
National premiere—National Festival of Australian Theatre, Canberra
Inkwings: Three Men Walk into a Bar (promenade site-specific theatre)
Family violence prevention project—Burnie, Tasmania

1996
Big *h*ART established as an incorporated, registered charity
Launched by Prime Minister John Howard at Parliament House, Canberra
Guns to Pens (hybrid theatre)
Crime prevention projects—tours: Tasmania, New South Wales, Canberra; performed inside juvenile justice centres

1997
SLR 5000 / 24 Hour Shift / Scissors Paper Rock Cereal (theatre)

Isolation and family violence prevention projects—West Coast Tasmania and Illawarra, NSW

1998
Hurt (community process begins)
Homelessness and youth-at-risk project—NSW, Tasmania

1999
Happy Water, Sad Water (outdoor dance installation)
Racism and water safety project—Manly Gallery, NSW

2000
Hurt (film)
Film premiere, AFI Award
Melbourne International Film Festival
Heaps of Rocks (installation)
Rural youth isolation project—west-coast Tasmania
Nuff Stuff, Wrong Way Go Back (hybrid theatre)
Juvenile justice and digital inclusion projects—Darwin, Northern Territory; performed in Don Dale Juvenile Justice Centre and Darwin Entertainment Centre
Big hART Works (hybrid theatre, installation, film)
Premiere performance—Adelaide Festival

2002
kNOT@Home (community process begins)
Homelessness, Indigenous and refugee youth project—NSW, Victoria, Western Australia, Tasmania

2003
Street Survivor (video game)
Homelessness project—Melbourne, Victoria

Sleep Well (installation performance)
Young mothers project—Bourke, NSW
Northcott Project (community process begins)
Public housing and social inclusion project—Sydney, NSW

2004
RU&I@1 (art installation)
Youth project—Hazelhurst Gallery Sutherland Shire, NSW
Chambers Crescent (community process)
Aboriginal youth project—Darwin, NT

2005
kNOT@Home (theatre and film performance)
Performance premiere—Melbourne International Arts Festival
LUCKY (multi-arts project)
Young mothers and social isolation project—north-west Tasmania
Radio Holiday and *Drive-in Holiday* (community process begins)
Young mothers and social isolation project—five isolated shack communities around Tasmania
Ngapartji Ngapartji (community process begins)
Aboriginal language and cultural rights project—Northern Territory and South Australia

2006
kNOT@Home (television series)
Eight-part series screened on SBS—national
Stickybricks: Northcott Project (outdoor theatre performance and feast)
Premiere performance—Sydney Festival

900 Neighbours: Northcott Project (film)
Documentary premiere—Sydney Film Festival
14 Stories: Northcott Project (short films)
ABC Screening—national broadcast
World Health Organisation Award
Safe communities: Northcott project—international
Ngapartji Ngapartji (theatre)
Premiere performance: national tour—Melbourne International Arts Festival
Junk Theory (community process begins)
Racism and social harmony project—Sutherland Shire, NSW
Ninti (online Pitjantjatjara language course launched)—international
Radio Holiday (radio, theatre and performance, mobile installation)
Premiere Federation Square, Melbourne—Melbourne International Arts Festival and isolated Tasmanian shack communities

2007
Drive-in Holiday (video, theatre and performance, mobile installation)
Premiere performance—Ten Days on the Island Festival, Tasmania, Hobart and isolated shack communities
GOLD (community process and multi-arts)
Drought and rural isolation project—NSW, Victoria, Queensland
This is Living (music theatre)
Ageing and intergenerational exchange project—Tasmania, statewide
Junk Theory (floating video and sound installation)

Premiere performance: Sydney Harbour—Sydney Festival

2008
DRIVE (community process begins)
Autocide and young men at risk project—north-west Tasmania

2009
Nyuntu Ngali (theatre)
Climate change project and young people—Northern Territory; Premiere performance—Adelaide, South Australia
Love Zombies (theatre)
Schools and creative industries project—north-west Tasmania
Namatjira (community process begins)
Cultural and Indigenous rights project—NT

2010
DRIVE (documentary)
Film premiere—Melbourne International Film Festival
Namatjira (theatre)
Premiere performance—Belvoir St Theatre, Sydney
2 Strong Hearts (hybrid theatre)
Schools and creative industries project—north-west Tasmania
Yijala Yala (community process begins)
Cultural heritage and digital inclusion project—Pilbara, Western Australia

2011
Smashed (short film competition)

Crime prevention and education project—north-west Tasmania
Nothing Rhymes with Ngapartji (documentary)
ABC film screening—national
NEOMAD (community process begins)
Aboriginal youth and cultural heritage project—Pilbara, Western Australia

2012
Namatjira (theatre and visual art)
National theatre tour—nationwide
We Vote Soon (TV studio installation)
Youth democracy project—north-west Tasmania

2013
Namatjira (theatre and visual art)
UK Season—London Southbank
Hipbone Sticking Out (theatre)
Premiere performance—Canberra Theatre Centre
MURRU (prison process begins)
Aboriginal justice and deaths in custody project—Pilbara, Western Australia
Museum of the Long Weekend (mobile caravan installation and performance project)
National inclusion and leisure project—Canberra
Blue Angel (community process begins)
Slavery at sea and fair shipping project—international
Samurai Digger (community process begins)
Peace, heritage and cultural exchange project—Canberra, ACT and Nara, Japan

2014
Acoustic Life of Sheds (community process begins)
Rural connection project—north-west Tasmania

To a Different Drum (percussion theatre project)
Schools and creative industries project—north-west Tasmania
Project Cosmopolitana (community process begins)
Social cohesion project—Cooma, NSW
SKATE (community process and showings)
Impact investment project—Melbourne
Namatjira to Now: 5 Generations of Watercolours (exhibition)
Exhibition opening: Parliament House, Canberra
Hipbone Sticking Out (theatre)
National tour—Melbourne International Arts Festival and Perth, WA
Murru Concert (concert–prison songs)
Opening—Melbourne International Arts Festival

2015

Blue Angel (hybrid theatre–multi-venue)
Premiere performance—Ten Days on the Island Festival, Tasmania
Ghosts in the Scheme (theatre)
Premiere performance—Canberra Theatre Centre
Acoustic Life of Sheds (site-specific concerts)
Premiere performance—Ten Days on the Island Festival, Tasmania

2016

Tjaabi (community process begins)
Cultural heritage and intergenerational exchange project—Pilbara Region, Western Australia
20+20 Project (skill building process)
Creative industries employment project—north-west Tasmania

Project O (hybrid public performance, video, art and installation)
Family violence prevention project—national locations

2017
Namatjira Project (feature documentary)
Premiere—Melbourne International Film Festival
This is Not a Speech Night (performance)
Schools and creative industries project—north-west Tasmania
John Pat Peace Place (outdoor installation and place-making)
Peace Garden opening—Roebourne, WA

2018
Tjaabi–Flood Country (hybrid music theatre)
Community showing—Pilbara Region, Western Australia
Songs for Peace (community concert and tea-making.
World premiere—Roebourne Pilbara Region, WA
Acoustic Life of Sheds
Wins National Art Music Award for Excellence in a regional area

COPYRIGHT INFORMATION

PLATFORM PAPERS
Quarterly essays from Currency House Inc.
Founding Editor: Dr John Golder
Editor: Katharine Brisbane
Currency House Inc. is a non-profit association and resource centre advocating the role of the performing arts in public life by research, debate and publication.

Postal address: PO Box 2270, Strawberry Hills, NSW 2012, Australia
Email: info@currencyhouse.org.au Tel: (02) 9319 4953
Website: www.currencyhouse.org.au Fax: (02) 9319 3649

ISBN 978-0-6484265-0-9
ISSN 1449-583X

Typeset in Garamond
Printed by Ligare Book Printers, Riverwood, NSW
Production by Currency Press Pty Ltd

FORTHCOMING

PP No.58, February 2019

THE CHANGING LANDSCAPE OF AUSTRALIAN DOCUMENTARY

Tom Zubrycki

In the evolving digital era, a new documentary landscape has emerged: new technology, expanding client base, but reduced government funding, and fragmented distribution. The old TV broadcast industry has re-structured itself; its diversity has narrowed. Presenter-driven series and reality programs have replaced one-off documentaries. Meanwhile, new global players such as Netflix and Amazon Prime are entering the Australian market. But outside the broadcast sector ambition and innovation are rising. Documentary filmmakers are finding new opportunities: relying less on traditional sources and gaining support from philanthropic foundations, crowd-funding, or simply self-funding.

Like finance, distribution is also more fragmented. Streaming and video-on-demand are not delivering much revenue to producers. Theatrical exhibition is diminishing; film festival screenings and cinema-on-demand increasingly important. The documentary will survive, writes Zubrycki: the makers' determination to tell our stories, and the audience's hunger for the real, will ensure that. 'We await the new dawn, but it's not here yet.'